HISTORICAL AGES

THE ARCHAIC PERIOD

BY HEATHER C. HUDAK

CONTENT CONSULTANT
Arthur Anderson, PhD
Associate Teaching Professor, Archaeology
School of Social and Behavioral Sciences
University of New England

Cover image: At the end of the Late Archaic Period, people began to grow crops. This change marked a shift to the Formative Period.

Core Library
An Imprint of Abdo Publishing
abdobooks.com

abdobooks.com

Published by Abdo Publishing, a division of ABDO, PO Box 398166, Minneapolis, Minnesota 55439.

Printed in the United States of America, North Mankato, Minnesota.
102024
012025

THIS BOOK CONTAINS RECYCLED MATERIALS

Cover Photo: North Wind Picture Archives/Alamy
Interior Photos: Jenny Ellerbe, 4–5; Red Line Editorial, 7; Jeffrey M. Frank/Shutterstock Images, 10; Daniel Eskridge/Shutterstock Images, 12; EWY Media/Shutterstock Images, 14–15, 45; Zack Frank/Shutterstock Images, 17; Zachary Frank/Alamy, 19, 43; Tom McHugh/Science Source, 22 (top left); Dr. Arthur Anderson, University of New England, 22 (top right); National Park Service, 22 (bottom left), 36; MET/BOT/Alamy, 22 (bottom right); Bebeto Matthews/AP Images, 24–25; Kevin Schafer/Photodisc/Getty Images, 26; Wolfgang Kaehler/Alamy, 29; Jon G. Fuller/VWPics/Alamy, 32–33; Imágenes del Perú/Moment Open/Getty Images, 34; Daniel Prudek/Shutterstock Images, 38; The Picture Art Collection/Alamy, 40

Editor: Laura Stickney
Series Designer: Ryan Gale

Library of Congress Control Number: 2024938491

Publisher's Cataloging-in-Publication Data

Names: Hudak, Heather C., author.
Title: The Archaic period / by Heather C. Hudak
Description: Minneapolis, Minnesota: ABDO Publishing, 2025 | Series: Historical ages | Includes online resources and index.
Identifiers: ISBN 9781098295615 (lib. bdg.) | ISBN 9798384916611 (ebook)
Subjects: LCSH: History, Ancient--Juvenile literature. | Land settlement--Juvenile literature. | Villages--Juvenile literature. | History--Juvenile literature. | Historical archaeology--Juvenile literature. | Civilization and science--Juvenile literature. | Anthropology, Prehistoric--Juvenile literature.
Classification: DDC 930.11--dc23

CONTENTS

CHAPTER ONE

MYSTERIOUS MOUNDS

Growing up, Reca Bamburg Jones had heard about three mysterious human-made mounds in the northern Louisiana forest not far from where she lived. The site was called Watson Brake. No one was sure exactly what the mounds were for. Later in life, Jones developed an interest in archaeology. She studied the subject at the University of Louisiana at Monroe.

One day in 1981, Jones was exploring Watson Brake. Willamette Industries Inc., a

Today, the Watson Brake mounds are covered by trees. Archaeologists continue to study the site.

foresting company, had cleared trees from the area. This made the land look very different. Jones noticed ridges connecting the mounds, which formed a circular shape. She realized that the mounds were actually ancient earthworks. Jones suspected they might be an important link to the past.

Jones worked with Harvard archaeologist John Belmont to map the site. The complex, located on the Ouachita River

SCIENCE MATTERS

More than 700 ancient mound sites have been discovered across Louisiana. In the 1980s, radiocarbon dating at mound sites in the southern United States showed that some sites were thousands of years old. But archaeologists weren't sure the results were accurate. They couldn't believe ancient people had built the mounds. Studies in the 1990s changed their perspectives. T. R. Kidder and other archaeologists explored Watson Brake in 1983. At the time, they decided that Watson Brake wasn't important. Later, Kidder said the 1990s studies challenged what people were seeing and helped them find correct answers.

THE WATSON BRAKE MOUNDS

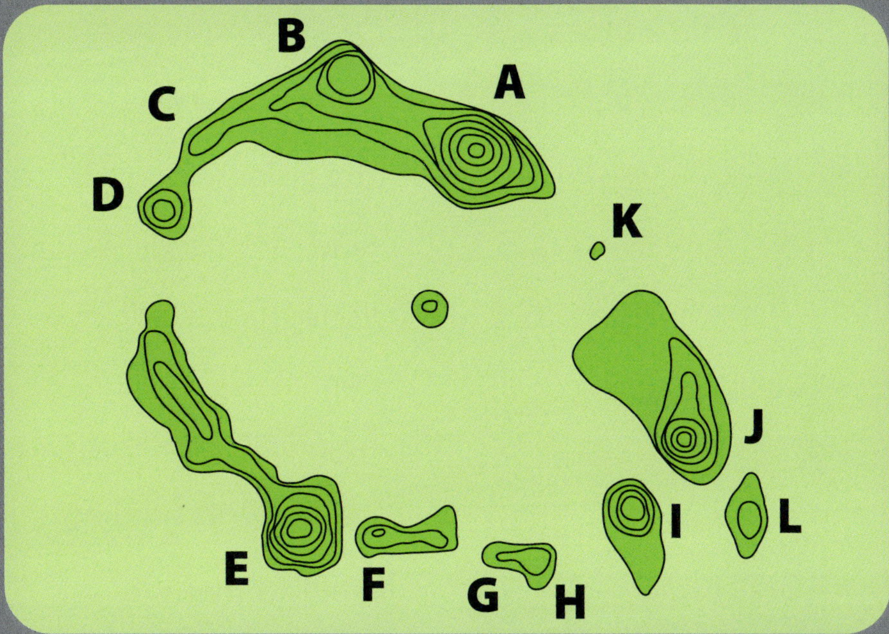

This map shows the sizes and positions of the mounds at Watson Brake. The mounds have different shapes and sizes. What do you notice about how the mounds are arranged? Why do you think the mounds were built this way?

floodplain near Monroe, Louisiana, measured about 300 yards (274 m) by 200 yards (183 m). It consisted of 11 earthen mounds. The smallest was about 1.6 feet (0.5 m) high. The largest stood 25 feet (8 m) tall.

In 1993, Jones teamed up with archaeologist Joe Saunders from Northeast Louisiana University. By then, Watson Brake was overgrown with forest again.

Jones and Saunders asked soil scientist Thurman Allen to take samples of soil from the largest mound. They used radiocarbon dating to see how old the soil was.

The results proved that the complex was built about 5,400 to 5,000 years ago, in what is known as the Archaic Period. This made Watson Brake one of the oldest ancient complexes in the Americas. Previously, many archaeologists thought Archaic peoples did not build such massive complexes. The rediscovery of Watson Brake contradicted that theory. Watson Brake predates Stonehenge in the United Kingdom and the Great Pyramids in Egypt. The Poverty Point World Heritage Site, which also features earthworks, is located only about an hour away from Watson Brake. It is three times Watson Brake's size, but it isn't as old.

Jones and Saunders weren't sure what Watson Brake was used for. They found artifacts, such as animal bones, shells, and stones, that provided some clues. But they could not uncover the exact purpose of the complex. At first, they thought it might have been used for burials or as a trade center. Another possibility was that mound building strengthened relationships between people or showed off their skills. Jones and Saunders believed hunter-gatherers likely used the site in summer and fall. It would have provided access to the Arkansas River, which flowed less than a mile away in ancient times.

Archaeologists believe ancient peoples lived at Watson Brake on and off for hundreds

POVERTY POINT

Poverty Point is one of the most significant archaeological sites in North America. It was built about 3,700 to 3,500 years ago by Archaic peoples living in what is now the Lower Mississippi River valley in northeastern Louisiana. The site is an earthen complex with large mounds, semicircular ridges, and a large flat area. No one knows exactly what Poverty Point was used for. It was likely part of a trading network. There is evidence that people might have lived at Poverty Point or held ceremonies there. In 1962, Poverty Point was declared a National Historic Landmark. It became a UNESCO World Heritage Site in 2014.

Archaeologists believe the Poverty Point earthworks were used for ceremonies and trade. Today, visitors can explore a hiking trail at the site.

of years. Over time, the path of the Arkansas River changed and was no longer as close to Watson Brake. People abandoned the site about 4,800 years ago. Today, the mounds remain off-limits to most people. Much of the complex is on private land, and tourists are not allowed to visit. The exact purpose of Watson Brake remains a mystery. But the mounds continue to help archaeologists better understand the lives of the people who built them.

TIME FOR CHANGE

Watson Brake was built during the Archaic Period. This is one of three major periods in American Indian prehistory. These periods took place before European people colonized the Americas. The Archaic Period is preceded by the Paleo-Indian Period (12,000 to 10,000 BCE) and followed by the Formative Period (1,000 BCE to 1450 CE). Not all experts agree on the dates of these periods. The dates can also vary by region. This is because different places entered the periods at different times.

The Archaic Period began in about 8,000 BCE. It was a time of transition. Earth began to change as ice thawed at the end of the last Ice Age. This period of cold global temperatures happened about 11,500 years ago. The cool, moist climate became warmer and drier. New plant life emerged. Thick evergreen forests and wetlands gave way to forests and grasslands. To adapt, plant-eating animals changed their feeding habits. Some migrated to other

Mammoths, *pictured*, had curvier tusks than mastodons. Mammoths also had a bony knob on top of their heads.

places to find food. Others, such as mastodons and mammoths, could not adapt and went extinct.

To survive in this new world, Early Archaic peoples had to adapt as well. The land was changing. Many animals that people relied on for food were gone. Life skills they had learned from their ancestors were not always useful and had to be adapted. People began to move and settle across the land. The Archaic Period marked a major change in how early people lived.

STRAIGHT TO THE SOURCE

Archaeologist Dr. Brad Lepper works with Ohio History Connection. He discussed common myths about Archaic mounds:

> *The Moundbuilder Myth refers primarily to 19th century interpretations of the mounds . . . of eastern North America as the works of a lost civilization unrelated to the American Indian cultures that inhabited this region at the time Europeans arrived on the scene. . . . The myth was based [on] the perceived contrast between the scale and remarkable sophistication of the ancient architecture . . . and the generally small-scale . . . American Indian societies then dwelling in the Ohio Valley. Historians largely have assumed the myth was created . . . to account for the presence of the amazing ancient earthworks, but also to cast the indigenous American Indians in the role of relatively recent intruders.*

Source: Brad Lepper. "The Moundbuilder Myth." *Ohio History Connection*, 5 June 2011, ohiohistory.org. Accessed 30 Apr. 2024.

BACK IT UP

The author of this passage is using evidence to support a point. Write a paragraph about the point the author is making. Then write down two or three pieces of evidence the author uses to make the point.

103396
103379
103379

CHAPTER TWO

EARLY ARCHAIC

The Early Archaic Period was the first subperiod of the Archaic Period. In North America, it lasted from about 8,000 BCE to 6,000 BCE. It was a time of transition from the Paleo-Indian Period that came before it.

Very little evidence of the Early Archaic has been found, so knowledge about the period is limited. However, the discovery of tools, burial sites, and social gathering sites has provided clues about how Early Archaic peoples lived.

Archaeologists have found more than 8,000 stone points at the Poverty Point site.

Early Archaic peoples of the Americas developed from the Paleo-Indian people. Like Paleo-Indians, Early Archaic peoples were hunter-gatherers. They moved with the seasons to find food and other resources, such as types of stone they could use to make tools.

CLIMATE CHANGE

During the Early Archaic, temperatures were higher than they had been in the past. There was more rain and snow. Sea levels began rising, and there were more wetlands. Many Early Archaic groups moved away from their lands after those lands were covered in water.

Most Early Archaic people likely lived in groups of about 20 to 50 members. Archaeologists believe that different groups gathered at certain times of year. They traded, held ceremonies, and tried to find spouses.

MOVING AROUND

Early Archaic people did not form permanent settlements. They stayed in one place for only a short

Some Early Archaic people lived in naturally occurring shelters such as caves or cliffs. The Russell Cave site in Alabama, for example, was once home to Archaic people.

amount of time. They hunted seasonal animals and gathered plants. People covered a small territory in which resources were plentiful. Often, their territory was near a river valley. This provided the group with water to drink and fish to eat.

People in the Early Archaic lived in simple homes, such as pit houses. These are types of dwellings built partly into the ground. The walls and roofs were often made of wood, mud, and grass. Examples have been

MEDICINE HOUSE

Medicine House is in the Hanna Basin near Hanna, Wyoming. It is one of the best-preserved pit houses from the Early Archaic. It is also one of the largest. Archaeologists have found evidence that Medicine House was used for shelter. People probably lived in it during the winter months. It was also used to store ricegrass seeds. Up to 40 percent of Medicine House has not been excavated.

found at sites such as Medicine House and Split Rock along the North Platte River in southern Wyoming. People also lived in rock shelters, which are overhanging cliff faces or caves used as shelter. These can be found in the Big Horn Mountains of northern Wyoming, in the Pryor Mountains of southern Montana, and along the Aurora branch of the Chagrin River in Cleveland, Ohio. Since Early Archaic peoples moved with the seasons, they lived in different types of shelters in different places. They built hearths to cook food.

Some of the best-preserved archaeological finds from the Early Archaic have been discovered

A life-size diorama at Russell Cave National Monument shows how the cave's early inhabitants might have lived.

in wetlands. In 1982, a construction worker was cleaning out a pond in Windover, Florida, when he dug up a human skull. Radiocarbon dating placed the skull at more than 7,000 years old.

Since then, archaeologists have found about 168 bog bodies at the site, which was once a prehistoric burial ground. The bodies had been buried under layers of peat, which created an oxygen- and acid-free environment that preserved them. Many of the bodies still had intact brain tissue. Scientists were able to study their DNA.

NAGPRA

Today, archaeologists do not excavate Indigenous burial sites without permission from the buried people's descendants. However, archaeologists in the past were not as respectful. They excavated human remains and displayed them in exhibits. In 1990, the US government passed the Native American Graves Protection and Repatriation Act (NAGPRA). This law said the remains of ancestors who had been excavated must be returned to their descendants, a process that is ongoing. The law also requires archaeologists to follow rules when investigating sites or handling human remains.

EATING HABITS

Paleo-Indians and Early Archaic peoples had different diets. Mammoths and other large animals from the Paleo-Indian Period did not live during the Archaic. But there was a wider range of food available in the Early Archaic than there had been during the Paleo-Indian Period.

Early Archaic peoples hunted smaller animals such as rabbits, bears, bison, deer, and elk. They also caught fish. Other peoples gathered berries, fruits, roots, nuts, and seeds.

Archaeologists believe Early Archaic men did most of the hunting, while women did the gathering. But the 2018 discovery of a 9,000-year-old female skeleton at Wilamaya Patjxa in Peru challenged that belief. The woman was buried with a hunting kit. In ancient times, people were typically buried with items they used in life. This meant the woman might have been a hunter.

TOOLS OF THE TRADE

Early Archaic peoples began developing tools to help them adapt to their changing environment and living conditions. One of the most common Early Archaic tools was the bifurcated base point. This type of stone point had notches on each side of the base. The notches were used to tie the point to a handle, which was likely made of wood.

A wooden tool called a spear thrower, or atlatl, made it easier to throw spears faster and farther. It consisted of a long pole with a notch or hook at the end. A spear was placed along the length of the pole,

PALEO-INDIAN VS. ARCHAIC TOOLS

PALEO-INDIAN

Spear points

Stone scraper

ARCHAIC

Spear points

Grooved axe

This graphic shows tools used by Paleo-Indian peoples and Archaic peoples. How are the tools different? How are they similar? Why do you think these tools changed over time?

with its end resting in the notch. A person held the pole in one hand and then launched it forward.

Stone points and other ancient tools have been found throughout the Americas. Most Archaic points had notches on the sides, corners, or base. These were likely used to tie the points to spears. Other Early

Archaic tools included stone axes and stone scrapers, which were used for preparing animal hides.

Early Archaic peoples used milling stones to grind seeds and roots into flour. Then they cooked the flour over hot rocks. They added meat and plants to it to make a porridge. People also made coiled baskets that were watertight and could hold food.

EXPLORE ONLINE

Chapter Two discusses the discovery of ancient artifacts and human remains. The website below provides more information about rules archaeologists must follow to treat these remains respectfully. What new information did you learn from the website? How is the information from the website the same as the information in Chapter Two?

NAGPRA

abdocorelibrary.com/archaic-period

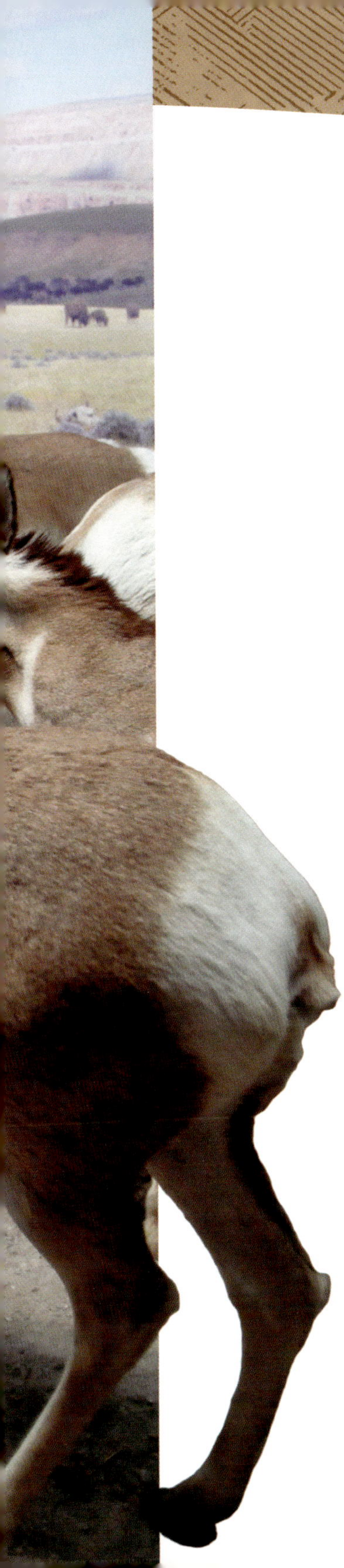

CHAPTER THREE

MIDDLE ARCHAIC

The Middle Archaic Period spanned from about 6,000 BCE to 4,000 BCE. Little is known about this period. During the Middle Archaic, the climate in some areas became much drier than it had been before. This created harsh living conditions for people. Temperatures were higher, and there was less rainfall.

During the Middle Archaic, people still lived as hunter-gatherers. They moved around with the seasons to take advantage

During the Middle Archaic, people frequently hunted animals such as pronghorn and bison. They also hunted deer, elk, and bighorn sheep.

Middle Archaic people in what is now the western United States gathered plants such as bitterroot. This flowering plant grows in dry soil and has edible roots. Archaic people cooked and ate them.

of resources available in different places. There were specific times of year for hunting and gathering different foods. For example, in Utah's Basin-Plateau, there was a specific time during which people moved to valleys in search of pronghorn, a deerlike animal. There were also times for gathering bitterroot and hunting squirrels, rabbits, and geese.

Middle Archaic people ate many of the same animals, nuts, berries, and fruit that Early Archaic people ate. In places such as the Gulf and Atlantic coastlines, Middle Archaic people collected shellfish in river valleys. Archaeologists have found shell middens, or mounds made of shells, across the Americas. Shell middens, such as those located at Timucuan Ecological & Historic Preserve in Florida and Cerro de las Conchas in Mexico, provide clues about how ancient peoples used shells and what types of shellfish they ate.

CERRO DE LAS CONCHAS

Cerro de las Conchas is a shell mound site on Mexico's south Pacific coast. It was created between 5,500 and 7,500 years ago during the Middle Archaic. It is one of the most studied sites from the period. It was used on and off year-round for processing shellfish. Evidence at the site suggests that marsh clams were people's main food source. Some shells at the site were unmarked, suggesting that people had steamed them open. Others were burned, suggesting they had been cooked as part of a clambake.

LIVING CONDITIONS

Most Middle Archaic sites, such as the Stanfield-Worley Bluff Shelter in Alabama, have more artifacts and evidence than Early Archaic sites. Archaeologists think this means that Middle Archaic peoples formed larger groups and had more objects to leave behind. They had smaller territories and lived in base camps. They likely built temporary shelters that were easy to move. They might have traded with people in other territories to get resources that were unavailable in their own territory.

At some Middle Archaic sites, archaeologists have found flaked stone tools made from local stones. This suggests that Middle Archaic peoples moved around less and did not travel as far as Early Archaic peoples, who often used stones from other locations to make tools. Middle Archaic people possibly spent at least part of the year in villages.

Remains of houses, camps, burial sites, and storage places have been found at some Middle Archaic sites. Archaeologists have also discovered skeletons with

At sites such as Edisto Beach State Park in South Carolina, visitors can hike past oyster shell middens. Archaeologists study the middens to learn more about how Archaic peoples in the area lived.

projectile points inside them. This provides evidence of warfare among Middle Archaic peoples. It's unclear what they fought over. One theory is that people fought over scarce resources due to the harsh climate.

EVOLVING TOOLS

Like Early Archaic peoples, Middle Archaic peoples created new tools and techniques to use in their changing environment. They developed a boiling stone to cook food. They used a tool called a pump drill to make a hole in a round, flat stone. Then they heated the stone in a fire. When the stone was hot, they used the hole to move it from the fire to a shallow pit in the ground. Inside the pit, there was a pouch made from animal skin that was filled with water or food, such as stew. The heat from the stone caused the contents of the pouch to boil.

Notched-stone net sinkers were another tool Middle Archaic people used. Net sinkers were made by carving a notch on opposite edges of a small, smooth stone. People used the

STANFIELD-WORLEY BLUFF SHELTER

The Stanfield-Worley Bluff Shelter is a sandstone shelter located about six miles (10 km) from the central Tennessee River valley in Colbert County, Alabama. Located under a rock wall, it is 55 feet (17 m) long and 250 feet (76 m) wide. Today, it is an archaeological site named after the people who own the properties around it. The Stanfield-Worley Bluff Shelter was excavated over three years in the 1960s. It contained artifacts dating from about 10,000 years ago to 1,000 years ago. Part of the shelter was used for burials during the Middle Archaic.

notches to attach the stone to a net or hook and line. The net sinker served as a weight, holding the net or line in place so people could catch fish. Archaeologists have found more than 800 net sinkers on a site in the Ouachita River drainage in Arkansas.

Another Middle Archaic tool was the mortar and pestle. It was used for crushing plants, seeds, and nuts. Bannerstones, or carefully shaped stones with holes drilled in them, were used as weights to balance atlatls.

FURTHER EVIDENCE

Chapter Three discusses how people developed and used tools during the Middle Archaic Period. What was one of the main points of this chapter? What evidence is included to support this point? Read the article at the website below. Does the information on the website support the main point of the chapter? Does it present new evidence?

FULL GROOVED AXES

abdocorelibrary.com/archaic-period

CHAPTER FOUR

LATE ARCHAIC

The Late Archaic Period lasted from about 4,000 to 1,000 BCE. There is much more evidence from the Late Archaic than the Middle Archaic. Around this time, the climate stabilized. It became similar to the climate that Europeans encountered when they first arrived in the Americas.

Late Archaic peoples lived as hunter-gatherers but also started growing their own food in gardens. They began to farm crops such as maize, squash, and sunflowers.

Archaeologists have found evidence that Late Archaic people grew a variety of crops. At the Caral-Supe site, ancient people ate maize, *pictured*, sweet potatoes, and squash.

Caral-Supe features well-preserved stone structures, plazas, and sunken courts. The ancient people who lived in Caral-Supe are sometimes called the Norte Chico.

Archaeologists have also found shell middens that suggest Late Archaic people ate shellfish. Stallings Island, a site in Georgia, features a shell midden from the Late Archaic.

During the Late Archaic, people began to build larger settlements. These settlements were often along riverbanks, such as the Tombigbee and Alabama Rivers in Alabama. Villages formed with smaller communities surrounding them. For example, large towns were developed at Poverty Point, while smaller communities branched out from the site. Other complex Late Archaic sites are in South America. One is Caral-Supe in Peru.

This city was built more than 5,000 years ago. It is the oldest-known center of civilization in the Americas.

SACRED CITY OF CARAL-SUPE

Caral-Supe is in the Supe Valley of Peru's Andes Mountains. Andean culture originated in this area around the same time that other cultures were developing in Egypt, China, and Mesopotamia. Caral-Supe stretched across 1,547 acres (626 ha) of desert. The massive complex included six large pyramids. UNESCO declared Caral-Supe a World Heritage Site in 2009. Archaeologists believe the site was used for trading or religious purposes.

HOUSING AND SOCIETY

After they started farming, Late Archaic peoples became less dependent on seasonal migration. They stayed in one place for a longer time. Because of this, they built more elaborate homes. They developed different styles of housing depending on their region. Few remains of Late Archaic homes have been found. Archaeologists think homes might have had shallow oval pits or cone-shaped

Some museums and national parks have replicas of Late Archaic dwellings, including wattle-and-daub homes, on display.

structures covered in hides. Others might have been similar to wigwams or wattle-and-daub buildings. Wattle-and-daub buildings are made of woven pieces of wood and mud or clay. During the Late Archaic, people also began building mound sites.

Archaeologists who study hunter-gatherers have found evidence that people were treated more equally in early societies than in many modern ones. The Green

River Valley Archaic region in Kentucky provides insight into Late Archaic societies. People likely lived in family groups of 15 to 20 people, including a mother, a father, and their children, as well as their children's spouses and children. There were no permanent leaders in these societies. Individuals with skills or knowledge served as leaders when needed. Everyone shared resources.

The Green River Valley region is home to one of the largest known Late Archaic burial sites. Some men, women, and children were buried with copper or bone pins and shell beads and pendants. Because of the way these people

STALLINGS ISLAND SITE

Stallings Island is a Late Archaic site. Ancient peoples used it from about 4,500 to 3,500 years ago. Stallings Island was home to a society of hunter-gatherers. The oldest-known pottery in North America was found at Stallings Island along with food remains, burial sites, and other artifacts. The site also has a 2-acre (0.8 ha) shell midden that is 10 feet (3 m) thick in some places.

Modern llamas and alpacas are descendants of the ancient llamas and alpacas raised by Late Archaic peoples.

were buried, archaeologists believe they might have been important figures in society. Archaeologists also discovered numerous dog burials in the Green River Valley, showing the special place that dogs held in Late Archaic society. During the period, people in the Andes also raised llamas and alpacas.

In the Late Archaic, territories became smaller, and boundaries between different groups became more defined. New languages and cultures developed too. Trade networks connected many groups. People traded tools and materials such as stones that were not available in their territories.

LATE ARCHAIC TOOLS

Late Archaic peoples made tools out of polished and chipped stone. They used bones to make needles and fishhooks. Late Archaic peoples in the Americas were also the first to use the bow and arrow. This tool made it easier to hunt large animals from a distance. Smaller arrow points than those used on atlatls have also been found across the Americas, including at Crawford Knoll in southwestern Ontario.

Toward the end of the Late Archaic, people moved around less. This meant they could have more belongings. In eastern North America, Late Archaic peoples carved bowls out of sandstone or steatite. They used the bowls for cooking.

In some places, archaeologists have found evidence that Late Archaic peoples made pottery. This practice marked the beginning of a transition to the next time

Many steatite bowls from the Late Archaic Period have handles and flat bottoms. Some may have been used for cooking or storing food.

period, the Formative Culture. At the end of the Archaic Culture, the way early people in the Americas lived changed. People began shifting away from societies of hunter-gatherers. Instead, they started settling in communities focused on farming.

The Archaic Period was an important time in history. New tools and ways of life developed as early peoples adapted to their changing environments. New cultures formed. These developments had a big effect on later historical periods. Archaeologists continue to uncover clues from the past, learning more about life during this pivotal period.

STRAIGHT TO THE SOURCE

In the 1990s, UNESCO began recognizing cultural landscapes, such as the Caral-Supe site. Dr. Shabnam Dailoo, assistant professor at Athabasca University, explains why:

> *A cultural landscape encompasses the natural history of a place as well as the cultural history of the people who associate with it. It is the physical base of a story about interaction between culture and nature. . . . Like a photograph holds an associated memory, a physical place anchors an intangible thing. To protect cultural landscapes is to keep telling stories.*

Source: Mike Donnelly and Todd Kristensen. "Blood Kettles and Buffalo Jumps: Communal Hunting on the Plains of Alberta." *RETROactive*, 8 June 2016, albertahistoricplaces.com. Accessed 3 Feb. 2024.

CONSIDER YOUR AUDIENCE

Adapt this passage for a different audience, such as your principal or friends. Write a blog post conveying this same information for the new audience. How does your post differ from the original text and why?

IMPORTANT DATES

10,000 BCE
The Paleo-Indian Period ends.

8,000 BCE
The Early Archaic Period begins in the Americas.

6,000 BCE
The Early Archaic Period ends, and the Middle Archaic Period begins.

4,000 BCE
The Middle Archaic period ends, and the Late Archaic Period begins.

1,000 BCE
The Late Archaic Period ends, and the Formative Period begins.

1981 CE
Archaeologist Reca Bamburg Jones explores the Watson Brake site in Louisiana and discovers an earthwork complex.

1982

People discover Early Archaic human remains preserved at a site in Windover, Florida. Archaeologists determine that the site was once a burial ground.

2014

Poverty Point, an Archaic earthwork site in Louisiana, becomes a UNESCO World Heritage Site.

2018

A 9,000-year-old female skeleton is found buried with a hunting kit at Wilamaya Patjxa in Peru.

STOP AND THINK

Tell the Tale

Chapter One of this book talks about the discovery of the Watson Brake site. Imagine you are rediscovering an ancient site from the Archaic Period. Write 200 words about your explorations of the site. How did you find the site? What artifacts do you find there? What clues do they provide about ancient peoples?

Surprise Me

Chapter Three discusses shell middens. After reading this book, what two or three facts about shell middens did you find most surprising? Write a few sentences about each fact. Why did you find each fact surprising?

Say What?

Studying historical ages can mean learning a lot of new vocabulary. Find five words in this book you've never heard before. Use a dictionary to find out what they mean. Then write the meanings in your own words and use each word in a new sentence.

Another View

This book talks about tools from the Archaic Period, such as stone points. As you know, every source is different. Ask a librarian or another adult to help you find another source about Archaic tools. Write a short essay comparing and contrasting the new source's point of view with that of this book's author. What is the point of view of each author? How are they similar and why? How are they different and why?

GLOSSARY

archaeology
the study of human history through artifacts and other remains

colonized
moved into and took control over an area

earthwork
a large, raised area made from piles of earth

excavate
to dig carefully out of the ground to uncover artifacts or remains

floodplain
a flat area of land that is frequently flooded

mastodon
a large ancient mammal that was similar to an elephant

migrate
to move from one place to another

peat
wet soil made of dead plants that can preserve things or be used as fuel

radiocarbon dating
a scientific method used to determine the age of organic materials

ONLINE RESOURCES

To learn more about the Archaic Period, visit our free resource websites below.

Core Library CONNECTION
FREE! COMMON CORE MULTIMEDIA RESOURCES

Visit **abdocorelibrary.com** or scan this QR code for free Common Core resources for teachers and students, including vetted activities, multimedia, and booklinks, for deeper subject comprehension.

Booklinks NONFICTION NETWORK
FREE! ONLINE NONFICTION RESOURCES

Visit **abdobooklinks.com** or scan this QR code for free additional online weblinks for further learning. These links are routinely monitored and updated to provide the most current information available.

LEARN MORE

Kaiser, Emma. *The Paleo-Indian Period*. Abdo, 2025.

Milosavljevich, Stefan. *Tales of Ancient Worlds.* Neon Squid, 2022.

Sockin, Caitlin. *Dig It! Archaeology for Kids*. Persnickety, 2023.

INDEX

About the Author

Heather C. Hudak has written hundreds of books for kids. When she's not writing, Heather enjoys traveling the world. She has been to about 60 countries. She has visited countless ancient sites, including the Acropolis in Greece, Angkor Wat in Cambodia, and Kohunlich in Mexico.